Y0-AVB-319

L E KING
IN concert

Album Art Direction: Larry Vigon
Photography: Catherine Wessel

CORPORATION

7777 W. BLUEMOUND RD. P.O. BOX 13819 MILWAUKEE, WI 53213

© 1994 SCREEN GEMS-EMI MUSIC INC. and COLGEMS-EMI MUSIC INC.
All Rights Reserved

Any duplication, adaptation or arrangement of the compositions
contained in this collection requires the written consent of the Publisher.
No part of this book may be photocopied or reproduced in any way without permission.
Unauthorized uses are an infringement of the U.S. Copyright Act and are punishable by Law.

CAROLE KING

When I was living in London in the early sixties, Carole King was a legend and a mystery to all of us. It seemed as if almost every time that we heard a brilliant new record out of America the song bore the Goffin/King credit that we had learned to revere and to trust.

When I came to New York and heard Carole's own demos of these same songs, I realized for the first time that this woman was not only a brilliant songwriter, but an exceptional singer as well. Finally, *Tapestry* came out and the rest of the world shared in this discovery and continues to do so.

The fruits of this unparalleled career have been the most extraordinary catalogue of songs that any one writer has ever assembled and a sublime and energetic skill as a performer.

Combining these two unique assets is the aim of this live album. Never has a musician had such an incredible list of songs from which to choose. "From Up on the Roof" to "You've Got a Friend," from "Natural Woman" to "So Far Away" to "Hold Out for Love," the songs span eras and styles in a remarkable and fascinating way.

Carole King does not tour very often, but when she does she throws herself into it heart and soul, anxious to make each performance as fresh and alive as possible. She has always been profoundly grateful to and appreciative of her band, comprising, as it does, some of the best musicians around, sometimes augmented by guests such as Slash from Guns 'n' Roses, who joins her on "Hold Out for Love" and "The Loco-Motion."

The order of songs on this album is taken directly from Carole's most recent concert tour and the intention was to capture the vigor, intensity and personality of a Carole King concert with both musical and emotional fidelity. Not only do I believe that this aim was achieved, but I further believe that those who have seen Carole in concert will treasure the recording as a perfect memento and those who have not will greatly enjoy sharing the experience now.

-Peter Asher, November 1993

IN concert

contents

HARD ROCK CAFE

Words and Music by
CAROLE KING

© 1977, 1994 COLGEMS-EMI MUSIC INC. and ELORAC MUSIC
All rights controlled and administered by COLGEMS-EMI MUSIC INC.
All Rights Reserved

11

12

Ca - fe.
Ca - fe.

I hope you can find— your way—
The reg - u - lars can't— keep a -

— to the Hard— Rock Ca - fe.
way from the Hard— Rock Ca -

fe.

Play 3x

UP ON THE ROOF

Words and Music by
GERRY GOFFIN and CAROLE KING

© 1962 (Renewed 1990) SCREEN GEMS-EMI MUSIC INC.
This arrangement © 1994 SCREEN GEMS-EMI MUSIC INC.
All Rights Reserved

SMACKWATER JACK

Words and Music by
GERRY GOFFIN and CAROLE KING

© 1971 SCREEN GEMS-EMI MUSIC INC.
This arrangement © 1994 COLGEMS-EMI MUSIC INC.
All Rights Reserved

SO FAR AWAY

Words and Music by
CAROLE KING

© 1971 COLGEMS-EMI MUSIC INC.
This arrangement © 1994 COLGEMS-EMI MUSIC INC.
All Rights Reserved

BEAUTIFUL

Words and Music by
CAROLE KING

© 1971 COLGEMS-EMI MUSIC INC.
This arrangement © 1994 COLGEMS-EMI MUSIC INC.
All Rights Reserved

34

(YOU MAKE ME FEEL LIKE) A NATURAL WOMAN

Words and Music by
GERRY GOFFIN,
CAROLE KING and JERRY WEXLER

© 1967 SCREEN GEMS-EMI MUSIC INC.
This arrangement © 1994 SCREEN GEMS-EMI MUSIC INC.
All Rights Reserved

HOLD OUT FOR LOVE

Words and Music by
CAROLE KING

Ev-ery-bod-y's got a lit-tle child in-side still look-ing for — love.

Ev-ery-thing we do is in — search of it, ev-ery-thing we say or think

© 1991, 1994 LUSHMOLE MUSIC
All Rights Reserved

WILL YOU LOVE ME TOMORROW?

Words and Music by
GERRY GOFFIN and CAROLE KING

© 1961 SCREEN GEMS-EMI MUSIC INC.
Copyright Renewed 1989
This arrangement © 1994 SCREEN GEMS-EMI MUSIC INC.
All Rights Reserved

JAZZMAN

Words and Music by
DAVID PALMER and CAROLE KING

Lift me, won't you lift me a-bove the old rou-tine.

Make it nice, play it clean, jazz - man.

(Alto sax-solo ad lib)

© 1974, 1994 COLGEMS-EMI MUSIC INC. & ELORAC MUSIC
All rights controlled and administered by COLGEMS-EMI MUSIC INC.
All Rights Reserved

take me down. — Jazz - man, come on, come on, come on, — come on, come on.

Repeat ad lib

(All band members trade in turn 16 bar ad lib solos)

rit.

IT'S TOO LATE

Words by
TONI STERN

Music by
CAROLE KING

© 1971 COLGEMS-EMI MUSIC INC.
This arrangement © 1994 COLGEMS-EMI MUSIC INC.
All Rights Reserved

CHAINS

Words and Music by
GERRY GOFFIN and CAROLE KING

© 1962 SCREEN GEMS-EMI MUSIC INC.
Copyright Renewed 1990 SCREEN GEMS-EMI MUSIC INC.
This arrangement © 1994 SCREEN GEMS-EMI MUSIC INC.
All Rights Reserved

66

I FEEL THE EARTH MOVE

Words and Music by
CAROLE KING

© 1971 COLGEMS-EMI MUSIC INC.
This arrangement © 1994 COLGEMS-EMI MUSIC INC.
All Rights Reserved

YOU'VE GOT A FRIEND

Words and Music by
CAROLE KING

© 1971 COLGEMS-EMI MUSIC INC.
This arrangement © 1994 COLGEMS-EMI MUSIC INC.
All Rights Reserved

THE LOCO-MOTION

Words and Music by
GERRY GOFFIN and CAROLE KING

© 1962 (Renewed 1990) SCREEN GEMS-EMI MUSIC INC.
This arrangement © 1994 SCREEN GEMS-EMI MUSIC INC.
All Rights Reserved